Health Wi̲_̲_̲ ̲_̲_̲_̲ ̲_̲_̲_̲_̲_̲_̲_̲_̲

A Simple Solution for Keeping or Getting
YOU
Healthy and Well
Faster, Quicker and Better

Fred Kienle

IF
You Change Your Attitude --- You Can Change Your Health

Because

No One Likes to be Sick…!

I will show You How
YOU
Can Play a Major Role in
Your Health and/or Recovery
In Whatever Health Issues You are Faced With

Copyright © 2021 by Fred D. Kienle

Without limiting the rights under copyright reserved above, no part of this publication may be reproduced, stored in or introduced into a retrieval system, or transmitted, in any form, or by any means (electronic, mechanical, photocopying, recording, or otherwise) without the prior written permission of the above author of this book. This is a work of fiction. Names, characters, places, brands, media, and incidents are either the product of the author's imagination or are used fictitiously. The author acknowledges the trademarked status and trademark owners of various products referenced in this work of fiction, which have been used without permission. The publication/use of these trademarks is not authorized, associated with, or sponsored by the trademark owners.

Dedication

To my wife Vivian
whose advice and support
are always there for me.
My Grandmother Eva Ruth Kienle
To All of the
"Treasured Seniors" That attend my
"Health With An Attitude" Seminars
For their Encouragement and Inspiration

Foreword

There is an old saying, "Attitude is everything," and I can tell you after being a mayor of one of the fastest growing cities in the United States of America for the past twelve years, a positive attitude goes a long way in surviving in today's political world at the local, state, and federal levels.

So, if a positive attitude and outlook in politics can help keep a person grounded and looking forward to a brighter future, then the same would be true when considering our health. My friend, Fred Kienle has tapped into something that everyone needs to read, learn, and apply in their lives.

I first became acquainted with Fred about a decade ago, when he attended some of our local chamber of commerce events. Then, to my surprise one Monday morning I had been scheduled to speak at the Zig Ziglar Corporation in Plano, Texas at one of their weekly devotionals, and Fred was there. In the ten years I have known Fred, he is the exact same person inside and out, as he was ten years ago. He is an encourager, motivator, and friend. I am left to assume it is because he daily applies the principals written in this book.

There are many things in life that we can't control. We can't control what our employer may do with their company; We can't control how that driver is going to react when we accidently pull out in front of him; We can't control genetics when it comes to our health; but with our attitude we can control how we face those challenges along the way…especially when it comes to living a healthier, happier, and longer life.

One of my mantras that I have adopted and promoted in my personal and professional life is the belief that, *"There are people who read about history and there are others who go out and make history."*

Dear reader, you need to pay close attention to the words of Fred Kienle, because he is an individual who is making history. The principals he had developed, supported, and taught in this book have made a difference in his life, and they can make a difference in your life too!

But don't take my word for it, turn the page and find out for yourself!

Eric Hogue,
Speaker, Author, Real Estate Agent
Mayor of Wylie, Texas
2008 – 2020

Endorsements

I am so Grateful to have such wonderful friends who took their time to read and endorse this book!

"From the 'Attitude Guru' himself -- Fred Kienle is *great attitude personified*! I know of no one better equipped to share about the influence of attitude than Fred. Plus, he writes from enough personal experience to be considered an authority. *Health With an Attitude* is perfect for today -- and tomorrow. It's full of encouragement and inspiration for everyone for whom good health is important."

Tom Ziglar,
Author, Speaker
President/CEO, Ziglar, Inc.,
and proud son of Zig Ziglar

"Fred has the ability to provide a much-needed perspective on attitude and the correlation between the mental and physical aspects of our lives. When he adds in the humor, it is just the cherry on top. Invest your time in reading this book and start your attitude toward better health now"

Mark Turner
Mayor: City of Wills Point, TX

"What a wonderful book! Fred Kienle knows his stuff and you should pay attention to the strategies in his new book. Sharing tips, stories, faith, and even humor, Fred will challenge you to rethink the role your attitude plays on your health. As he states: 'Change Your Attitude – Change Your Life.' Not only do I recommend this book, but you should also schedule a seminar with Fred to experience his contagious attitude!"

Mike Rodriguez
Pro Speaker, Master Trainer,
Best Selling Author
CEO, Mike Rodriguez International LLC

"If you want to change your life, then it starts with your attitude! In **Health With An Attitude**, author Fred Kienle shares insightful strategies to help you to live your best life personally and professionally. His enthusiasm is contagious and you'll be inspired, motivated, and ready to take on a whole new attitude after reading this book. If you're ready to reach new levels of success in life, then I highly recommend you read this book."

Michelle Prince: www.MichellePrince.com
Speaker, Best Selling Author & Publisher
Author of "Winning In Life Now", "Busy Being Busy", "The Power of AUTHORITY"

When you read Fred Kienle's book, "Health with an Attitude," several things will happen, almost immediately. One is that you will know how to improve your health and improve the health of those around you. Not by some new drug, supplement, or exercise, but by the power of the mind to focus on what is really important in your life – your health! Fred is not the normal health coach who says to do this and that and your world will change. He combines the psychological function of thinking with personal choices that have worked for hundreds of years.

"Health with an Attitude" is positive and uplifting, merging wit, humor, personal stories, quotes, and success stories masterfully written to encourage the reader to want to read more and more. There are many 'must-read' books in the marketplace – this is one that should be in the 'top ten' must-read for personal health improvement.

Fred's personal story-telling style gives the reader a sense of fulfillment knowing that improvement is within easy grasp. It is impossible to read "Health with an Attitude" and not smile! Change your mindset with the easy roadmap that Fred provides and your world will be different sooner than you think.

Red O'Laughlin
Best Selling Author, Public Speaker, Independent Publisher
Author of "Longevity Secrets for Healthy Living" and "The Joy of Ageless Health"

"This is a powerful book for the times we are living in. Fred Kienle artfully reminds readers the vital importance our attitude has on our health.

"Health With An Attitude" should come with a highlighter! It is chock full of live enhancing points and tips. Read and live this book!!"

Dean Lindsay
Award Winning Author, Keynote Speaker, Business Consultant
Author of "Creating Progress in a World of Change," "Big PHAT Goals"
Deanlindsay.com

"As a U.S. Olympian and former professional football player, I learned early on that ATTITUDE is EVERYTHING! *Health with an Attitude* provides a framework that you and I can tap into immediately when it comes to controlling our attitude which is so closely tied to our health and wellbeing. This book is the guide you need to live the life you want...!

Johnny Quinn,
U.S. Olympian (Bobsled)
Author and Keynote Speaker

Introduction

Today is March 30, 2020

Our nation along with the entire world has been turned upside-down by an invisible enemy called **COVID-19 Pandemic.** It has definitely changed our daily lives and set all of us on our rear ends. As I finish writing and publishing this book, I know, that by the Grace of GOD, we will be past this World-Wide Crisis. I also know, that during this event, WE will all begin to take a critical and hard look at how we approach our health and its true worth to ourselves, our families and our fellow man...!

Over the last several years, I have been presenting a seminar titled "Health With An Attitude" to Hundreds of our "Treasured Seniors" at over 200 Assisted Living Homes and Retirement Communities. My beginning statement is one that my grandmother would always say, **"Son, if you have your Health, you have EVERYTHING...!"** Well, at the time she told me this bit of elderly wisdom, I was a young lad about 14 years old and it did not make any sense to me whatsoever...because I could jump out of bed, jump into my clothes, jump on my bike and go roller-skating, etc....!!! Little did I truly understand what roll my overall Health played in my everyday life.

As I grew older and started to actually observe how Health affected me as well as everyone at different stages of their lives, I began to realize how vital our health plays in our everyday events. As I looked back over my 75 years of life, I can see where I could have made numerous small changes in my basic hygiene, eating and exercise habits that would have made some Monumental and Positive effects on my body and overall health. I have also come to realize that one of the most compelling overall things that a person can do to drastically improve their health, is to have a Fantastic Positive Attitude concerning all of the above...!

WHAT...???

How can an Attitude be more important than: Diet, Exercise, Hygiene, etc...???

Because...!!!

Your Attitude WILL determine HOW WELL you will accomplish all of these items on your Staying Healthy List.

I have been blessed with a wonderful positive attitude and it has helped me throughout my entire life. I know how important a person's attitude is in everything they think, do and say. If you have a negative attitude it will affect all you do in a negative and non-productive way…if you have a positive attitude it will affect all you do in a positive way…!!! One of my favorite quotes is **"Change Your Attitude – Change Your Life"** I have approached all my seminars with a focus on this basic principal. I don't care if it is about Safety, Faith, Leadership or pick any subject you want, your attitude will enter into every fiber of every one of them.

I know my preaching about having a good attitude toward their health to these seniors, has had a positive and profound effect on so many of them. It has been a blessing to me when I am invited to do a return visit to these Assisted Living Homes and hear these seniors tell me the great results that they have experienced by practicing what I have asked them to do about changing their attitudes.

Since you have already picked up this book and have read this far, I encourage you finish reading to the end and apply some of these basic changes, thoughts and principals to your health, your life and the loved ones around you. Because YOUR health is not only important to you but to your spouse, kids, parents, and friends in your life.

I have made this book simple; each chapter is short, entertaining and easy to read, knowing that it will inspire and motivate you to a life of better health. I believe that Laughter and Humor is one of the best Medicine's available to everyone, I hope you will take a moment to read each "Time to Laugh" at the end of each chapter. They contain a Humorous Story that will put a smile on your face.

I wish all of You, Blessed Health in all You do.

Regards,

Fred Kienle

Table Of Contents

Chapter One

My Grandmother always said:

"Son, If You have Your Health You have Everything…!"

She told me that when I was a 14-year-old boy…and you know what…it didn't make A-Lick-Of-Sense to me what-so-ever. I couldn't fathom what she was getting at because at 14, I could jump out of bed, jump on my bike, roller-skate, do somersaults and do all kinds of things…to me health wasn't an issue. I explained to her the important things to me, as a 14-year-old boy were:
**Making lots of money…!
Getting my driver's license and fast cars…!
And of course, as a boy of 14
Cute Girls…!!!!**

She would just sigh and shake her head…knowing that I didn't understand what she was trying to explain to me.

HOWEVER!

As I got older and started paying a little more attention to other age groups around me, I began to notice a difference in what they could or could not do. I also began to notice that what they could or could not do, was NOT always attributed to their age.

The revelation of what people
Could or Could Not Do
HIT ME

Health was not always about age
It was usually related to

The <u>Condition</u> of a Person's Health at Any Age

Wow…! Now I began to realize that
Good Health is a Blessing

It's about:

**Freedom
Independence
Being able to go and do the things you want to do
Without the need to always depend on someone else to help you**

My perception of a person's health began to go through some changes. I began to notice a difference in the people that were always moaning and complaining as opposed to those that had a smile on their face and nice things to say.

"Hmmm…!"
I wondered, "What made the difference…?"

While greeting someone, have you ever asked them, "How are you doing today…? And WISHED YOU HAD NEVER ASKED…??? I'll bet you dollars to donuts you have. When you ask that question, I have found out that Soooooo many people will Unload on you all their aches, pains and problems. They will describe to you every disease and ailment they have ever had. Not only that, they will also let you know all the health issues their Aunt Matilda, Uncle Harry and their pet dog have. They don't seem to have ONE Positive thing to say about their Health. As I watch the people that answer with this negative response, I also notice they are usually less healthy and tend to look older than they are.

On the other hand, the ones you approach that had a spring in their step with a firm handshake, and would usually respond with a Positive answer like;
**Never felt better
Fit as a Fiddle
Finer than a Frogs Hair
Or as Zig Ziglar would always answer,
"Better than Good"**
They seemed to be in better health, looked younger and have a purpose for living.

"Could it be that simple...?"
I once again, questioned myself.
"Could a person's everyday attitude have that much of a profound effect on their health...?"

So, as I started to study this simple scenario, here is what began to surface and become extremely obvious.

Let me call my first study group "The Hand Wringers & Whiners." These folks are made up of all different ages. Sometimes starting in their teens all the way up to folks in their 80's and 90's. They usually have a negative outlook on just about everything. They shuffle through life and their conversation usually consists of saying things like:

1. I'd be alright if it wasn't for this (name any disease)
2. I knew something bad would happen.
3. Everyone else gets a break except me.
4. Why am I always sick?
5. I'll never get a raise of promotion.
6. I'll never get well.
7. I always have bad luck.
8. Bla, Bla, Bla...!

You know the rhetoric...and it never ends...they will paint a dark cloud for you, even on the sunniest day. If you are not careful, they can bring you down with them...So, keep a smile on your face and (without being rude) get away from them as quickly as you can.

If you really take notice, these folks that whine, complain and seem bitter all the time, are usually not in the best of health. They seem to look and act Much Older than they really are.

While on the other hand, the next study group, which I have identified as "The Doer's & Smilers" their approach to everything is 180 degrees apart from the first group. And their ages are also from the teens on into their 80's, 90's and in this group even 100 plus...! They seem to stride through life with a Spring in their step and a Smile on their face. They say things like:

1. This is a wonderful morning.
2. I KNOW I will get through this illness.
3. I am going to have a Great Day.
4. I am so fortunate.
5. We will get through these tough times.
6. I am Healthy

This type of self-talk is what will keep, not only them happy, but all the folks around them happy. These folks are like magnets and will attract more people around them and not repel them. Again, if you take notice, these folks always seem to be in Better Health and usually look so Much Younger than they really are. Not only that but they seem to say these positive affirmations, even if they are not feeling good…Hmmm…!

And this my friend, is all attributed to their ATTITUDE toward life, health, family & job.

That really got me to thinking about how important and related an attitude is toward a person's health. I am and have always been convinced that a person's attitude is important in just about everything we do in life. I published a book titled "Success With An Attitude" and it revolves around 10 key personal skills that are unquestionably tied to their attitude. I conduct numerous seminars:

"Success With An Attitude"
"Safety With An Attitude"
"Health With An Attitude"
"Faith With An Attitude"
"Laughing With An Attitude"
"Gratitude With An Attitude"
"Leadership With An Attitude"

Every one of these seminars revolve around my belief in the fact that
"Everything begins with An Attitude"

I ask everyone at the beginning of each of these seminars, "How many of you came in here with an attitude?" Most everyone will raise their hand and I tell them, "Yep, you came in with one, whether it is a Good, Bad or Indifferent one…You did come in with one."

Then I tell them the one you came in with was entirely up to them because...

"THEY HAD A CHOICE"
"Change Your Attitude – Change Your Life"

I then ask them:

**"If You Knew You Could Positively Improve Your Health
simply by
Changing Your Attitude...
Wouldn't You Do It...?"**

Guess what 99% of them said...??? You Betcha...They said **YES**...!

My grandmother knew how important her health was but even in the wisdom of her age and words, she didn't really understand the importance her attitude played in her own health. She had a few health issues but luckily, she had a pretty fair attitude and a decent positive outlook on life and lived to the age of 81.

Below is a statement that will help you focus on what I am trying to INSPIRE every one of you to understand.
I believe that if her Self-Talk and Attitude had been more Positive and Encouraging, she would have lived Even Healthier and Longer than just to 81.

This is not just a statement that I am throwing out to you lightly, but one that has been studied, observed and looked at for over 10 plus years. *See my Mission Statement in the next chapter.*

Time to Laugh

22-Year-Old Wife:

I was walking through my favorite park yesterday and I came upon an elderly gentleman sitting on one of the benches. He was sobbing uncontrollably. Certainly, I was concerned, so I stopped and asked why he was so depressed and sad. He collected himself and explained that he was 93 years old and at home he had an extremely beautiful 22-year-old wife that loved him dearly. She cooked, cleaned and romantically adored him completely. Confused, I asked him, "Sir, if you have a 22-year young wife that adores you so completely…Why are you Crying?" His sobs became overwhelming loud as he answered, "I can't remember where I live…!"

Attitude Thought #1
> "If You Knew You Could Positively Improve Your Health Simply by Changing Your Attitude… Wouldn't You Do It…?"

Chapter Two

My Mission

"Why this should have an impact on every one"

> **My Mission**
> Is to define, convince, encourage, and motivate: every patient, every medical professional and basically every person I can, to understand how important their attitude is towards their life long health or recuperating and achieving a healed and healthier body… faster, quicker and better than expected.
> **Fred Kienle**

So, with that statement said, let me explain a little further and tell you why I feel that a person's attitude is more important than you could ever imagine.

For several weeks, every Friday morning, at 5:30 AM, I would drag my, not so awake, body out of bed, get dressed and drive to a Large Training Hospital in the Dallas downtown area. At 7:30 AM a notable Doctor of Oncology, from all across the nation, would present a 1-hour lecture on the subject of Cancer. The lecture hall would be full of Doctors, Interns, Nurses, etc. (and sleepy me)

I would studiously listen and take notes...but honestly, the subject matter was so far over my head that I understood --- Maybe 5%...! The real reason that I attended these lectures was to interview the doctor after his/her presentation. I would ask only ONE Question:

**"In all the patients you have treated,
How important is their attitude in their battle with cancer?"**

Would you believe it if I told you their answer, without hesitation, was basically this?

The patient's attitude is so paramount and plays such a vital role in their approach to treatment. The ones that have a Strong Positive Attitude and a Will to Fight, usually recover Faster, Quicker and More Completely than those with a Negative Attitude.

Wow...! Their response was so unanimous and definitive that it encouraged me to interview more General MD's, Nurses, Dentists, etc. Guess what...? They all answered with the same basic response.

So, these interviews alone should encourage you to read on and understand the importance of having a Positive Attitude and How to maintain it. It's truly pretty simple:

The GOOD thing about it is ---

It's totally up to you...!

The BAD thing about it is ---
It's Totally up to YOU...!

With that in mind I will walk you through some examples, thoughts and scenarios, you can put into practice which will help you to experience a Stronger Positive Attitude along with steps in how to maintain it.

Just think, when you woke up this morning you had an attitude (Good, Bad or Indifferent) ...RIGHT? So, whatever that attitude was you also had a choice to either "Live with It" OR "Change It."

An attitude is more contagious than the worst Virus known to mankind...it will infect everyone that you come into contact with and they, in turn, will infect others ALL DAY LONG... until someone Changes their Attitude.

Have you ever tossed a pebble into a pond or pool of water and watched all the ripples flow outward from the point of impact? They seem to be endless and touch every bank of the pond. That is exactly what YOUR attitude will do to everyone around you.

Don't get me wrong...I know that you can't wake up every morning in a GREAT MOOD, with everything "Coming Up Roses." We all face challenges and problems in our everyday lives. Some days just start off "Not So Good" we have aches, pains, health issues, financial worries, relationship issues...and on and on. You will infect your friends and loved ones with your positive or negative attitude that you start with. However, I want to encourage you that;

YOU HAVE A CHOICE...!
You Can Change Your Attitude

Sounds simple and I have had so many people tell me, "Fred, you don't understand what I am going though!" I will always tell them that they really need to take whatever issue they are having and change the way they approach it. I like to use this quote from Joyce Meyer.

"Life May give you a Cactus
But
You Don't Have to Sit on It...!"

Problems and issues show up every day and we have to face them, whether we like it or not. I want to leave this chapter with this extremely important fact:

"The attitude you have when you tackle these issues and problems, WILL determine the success you will have in conquering them...!"
Fred Kienle

Time to Laugh

Baseball Buddies:

    Pat and Mike were avid baseball fans and even since they were little tyke's, they were true Baseball Buddies. They loved baseball so much that they went to every game they could and to every stadium just to watch baseball. As they grew older, they wondered if, there was Baseball in Heaven? So, they shook hand and made a pact, that whoever passed away first and went to Heaven, must find a way to come back and let the other one know if there is Baseball In Heaven. Well, sadly enough, two weeks later Patty passed on and went to Heaven. Mike was so sad and lonely because he lost, not only his best friend, but his Baseball Buddy as well. One day as Mike was out for a walk, "POOF...!" Suddenly, Patty appeared right in front of him! He was glowing, had wings on his back, a halo on his head and he was an Angel...! Mike exclaimed loudly, "O Patty my friend, you've come back, do you have any news for me?" Patty replied, "Yes Mike, I have some Good News and I have some Bad News...!" Mike said, "O Patty, tell me the Good News first." "Well" Patty said happily, "There is Baseball in Heaven...!" Mike jumped with glee and said, "That's wonderful Patty, I'm so glad...Now, what's the Bad

News...? Patty smiled and said, "Mike, Tomorrow, YOUR PITCHIN...!!!"

Attitude Thought #2

> You are the Pebble in the Pond
> Which way do you want your ripples
> to infect yourself, your family and your friends?
> You, and You alone have the Choice...!

Chapter Three

Bring Yourself into the Healing Process

"Today be thankful and think how rich you are. Your family is priceless, your time is gold and your health is wealth."
Zig Ziglar

Most everyone who is reading this book has a Primary Physician or Doctor that they can go to for their health, checkups and wellness issues. I want to take a minute and thank every one of these medical professionals. They not only see to our health and well fair during normal everyday circumstances...when needed the surgeons perform wonderful healing operations on our bodies. My appreciation and heart truly go out to all of these FRONT LINE

HEROS during this COVID-19 Pandemic Event. They are true hero's and deserve our deepest respect and honor.

Let's face it, there are so many of these wonderful medical professionals that are responsible for the diagnosis, curing and healing process of the human race.

BUT

Along with these wonderful professionals

YOU

Need to bring yourself into the Healing Process as Well…!

I want to establish an irreversible reason for you to have a positive and unfailing approach and attitude toward your Health, Healing and Well-being.

Because YOU

Will Play a Major Part in Your Recovery
And It Will Be Up to You and Your Attitude
In How Successfully You Handle the Healing
Of Whatever Health Issues You are Faced With

To many times we become so totally dependent on these professionals to solve and fix our health issues that we, as individuals, fail to see the activities that each one of us should be participating in, to help ourselves get well. When we are ill, we tend to have the complacent attitude that it is "Up to the Doctor" to get us healthy and all we have to do is get a shot, take the pills, get plenty of rest and drink plenty of fluids. This is all great advice but each one of us can, could and should do SO MUCH MORE…!

You're probably asking me, "Well, isn't that what doctors are supposed to do...?" and I will agree with you to a point, however, I also know for a fact that YOU can become a crucial part in how you approach the treatments that your doctor prescribes for you. Let me explain this a little further.

Over the last 3 years, I have performed my "Health With An Attitude" seminars in over 200 Assisted Living Homes and Retirement Centers. After each presentation, I love to sit and listen to these "Treasured Seniors" tell me their stories, which are full of wisdom, knowledge and history. In these memorable chats, I have talked to numerous seniors that are facing critical health issues. Some with cancer, heart conditions, diabetes, arthritis and other serious health ailments. I have personally witnessed a huge difference which was this:

THE
CONDITION OF THEIR HEALTH
WAS NOT NECESSAIRLY RELATED TO THEIR AGE
BUT
WAS PROPORTIONALLY RELATED TO
THE
CONDITION OF THEIR ATTITUDE...!

Even I was amazed that health was not necessarily related to their age. I am 75 and there were many that were younger than myself that acted and looked much older than me. On the other hand, there were many that were older than myself that acted and looked much younger than me. Hmmm...! The point that I will continually try to impress upon everyone is how important an attitude is in a person's total health, at **any** age.

It does not take long in a conversation, to tell what direction a person's attitude tends to lean. It truly is as simple as telling me if they see the proverbial glass of water that is filled exactly to the halfway mark. Is it Half Full or Half Empty? A person's phrasing and words that they use to talk about themselves or their issues, will always define the way they approach life and how their attitude effects it.

Please, don't get me wrong…I realize that there are health conditions that people have which are seriously devastating, and your attitude and positive thinking will not be the cure all answer to these issues. However, I would like for you to consider this quote from Zig Ziglar and understand the true meaning of his words.

> ***"Positive Thinking will not allow you to do Everything,***
> ***But it will allow you to do Everything***
> ***BETTER***
> ***than Negative Thinking will."***
> *Zig Ziglar*

This is why your attitude is so important in whatever health issues you are facing or will face in the future. The attitude and state of mind that you will use to confront the treatments, surgeries, therapy and recommendations that your physician prescribes to you, WILL have a dramatic effect on the outcome of your recovery. Let's face it, when your attitude is down in the dumps, bitter and negative your immune system is usually affected. Recent studies show that severe prolonged stress and chronic negative thinking can compromise the immune system. By the same token, studies have also revealed that individuals with a positive attitude toward life tend to become sick less often than those with a negative attitude.

A John Hopkins report states: *People with a family history of heart disease who also had a positive outlook were one-third less likely to have a heart attack or other cardiovascular event within five to 25 years than those with a more negative outlook.*

Our first line of defense is our immune system. Approximately 80% of our gut is our immune system. It is critical to eat healthy, exercise, sleep well, reduce stress as well as the normal protective measures we do daily. Being healthy and staying healthy is not a passive activity…you have to constantly be in a positive mindset to battle your disease, regardless of what it is. Don't just sit idly by and allow your condition to take over your mind and attitude.

I encourage you to never view your health issue or illness as a permanent condition.

I have had so many people ask me, "What kind of things are we doing with our attitudes that are counterproductive to our health?" Here is an extremely simple example of how you effect your healing procedure. Let's say a doctor prescribes a prescription for you to take twice a day. Do you ever hear yourself or others say out loud, "These pills are probably not doing me any good?" OUCH…with that negative affirmation, you have just set up your body and your brain for some resistance to these pills. When you make affirmation's out loud, either positive or negative, they have an effect on your mind and body. What you should say out loud are statements like, "Wow…! These pills are really working and making me feel better every time I take them…!"

I have asked several physicians this question, "Do you ever tell your patients to say out loud?" - 'These pills are really working and making me feel better every time I take them…!" Every one of them answered "No." So I asked them "Why Not?" They usually answer me with this, "I didn't think it was necessary." After a brief conversation about it, a light seems to come on in their eyes and they have all said they could see how the combination of the Pill and Positive Affirmations could benefit their patients.

Well, you can take this exact same approach to every single health issue that you have.

If You Change Your Attitude – You can Change Your Health

I have talked to numerous seniors that have battled or are battling cancer, they have all told me the horror and fear of going through Chemotherapy and Radiation Treatments. Since I have never experienced them, I can only surmise the atrocities of how bad it makes them feel. One of my favorite conversations was with a lady that has overcome some serious cancer tumors. She told me that she knew what the Chemotherapy and Radiation Treatments was going to do to her body. She knew she was going to feel extreme nausea, how weak she was going to feel and to add insult to injury, the loss of her precious hair. Her secret to overcoming all of this incredible negativity was her Impressive Positive Attitude. Before she would go into these Treatments, she would put on, what she called her "Positive Smile" square her shoulders, stand up straight and tell herself **Out Loud** things like:

1. These treatments WILL defeat this cancer…!
2. I WILL recover from the ill effects of these treatments quickly…!
3. My body WILL have a Positive Response to these treatments…!
4. I WILL regain my strength right away…!
5. My hair will grow back real soon…!

Guess what? She DID defeat the cancer; she DID recover from each ill effect and she DID regain her strength quicker than normal. Not only that but, her hair did grow back. Her doctors told her that she was a great patient and her attitude went a long way in helping her recover faster and with less ill effects than other patients with a negative approach to these treatments. So….!

The Attitude and State of Mind that you will use to confront any of the Treatments, Surgeries, Therapy and Recommendations that your physician prescribes to you, WILL
have a dramatic effect on the Outcome and Success of Your Recovery

A positive attitude and saying positive affirmation's out loud help to reduce stress, worry, fear and anxiety. When these negative symptoms are taken away or at least reduced, your body's immune system will be in a better position to help your body focus and work on the actual health issue at hand.

Later in Chapter 7, I will tell you more about positive affirmations with examples and how to use them.

Time to Laugh

Father O'Malley

There I was sitting quietly at the bar at me favorite Pub, having a nice Pint of Guinness Beer. Suddenly, Father O'Malley busted into the Pub. Surveying the entire place with a critical eye he called out to one of the patrons and said, "Hey, O'Leary, Do you want to go to Heaven?" and O'Leary replied, "O yes Father, I do want to go to Heaven." Then Father O'Malley pointed and told him to go over and stand against the wall. O'Leary quickly got up and went over and stood against the wall. As Father O'Malley looked over the pub again and called out to another, "O'Hare, do you want to go to Heaven?" and of course he answered, "O yes Father, I definitely want go to Heaven." Then Father O'Malley pointed and told him to also go over and stand against the wall. O'Hare quickly got up and went over and stood against the wall along side of O'Leary. Then Father O'Malley's gaze fell on me sitting at the bar. He called out, "Freddy, Do YOU want to go to Heaven?" of which I promptly replied, "NO…!" Shocked Father O'Malley asked, "What do you mean NO? …Freddy, when you die, don't you want to go to Heaven?" After taking another sip of me beer I replied, "O Sure Father, I certainly do want to go Heaven when I die…**I thought you were getting a group together to go NOW…!**"

Attitude Thought #3

> **The Attitude and State of Mind that You use to confront any of the**
> **Treatments, Surgeries, Therapy and Recommendations**
> **Your physician prescribes for You,**
> **WILL**
> **Have a dramatic effect on the Outcome and Success of Your Recovery**

Chapter Four

Laughter is the Best Medicine

"The old man laughed loud and joyously,
Shook up the details of his anatomy from head to foot,
And ended by saying
That such a laugh was money in a man's pocket,
Because it cut down the doctor's bills like everything."
Mark Twain

George R.R. Martin, the author of "Game of Thrones" said this, "Laughter is Poison to Fear…!" I wholeheartedly agree and compare it to Light as opposed to Darkness.

It was stated in Luke 8:16 (KJV)
16 No man, when he hath lighted a candle, covereth it with a vessel, or putteth it under a bed; but setteth it on a candlestick, that they which enter in may see the light.

When you are in a good mood and have laughter on your lips, the fear, depression, anxiety and worry will disappear just as darkness will disappear when you light one small candle. A study revealed that:

One Minute of Anger Weakens the Immune System for 4 to 5 Hours
But
One Minute of Laughter Boosts the Immune System for 24 Hours

Have you ever noticed when something has really made you angry, you get that ugly feeling that remains deep in your gut won't go away for several hours? I think that you already are beginning to understand…that is so detrimental to your immune system and it keeps your entire body out of whack for quite some time.

So, let me ask you one question? Which one would you choose – Anger or Laughter? If you're in a bad mood, stressed, depressed, anxious, fearful etc. Isn't your health important enough for you to try your darndest, to change your attitude to a positive one? Well, Laughter is one of the best ways to lift your spirits and change your mood.

Bob Hope, one of our favorite iconic comedians, lived to be 100 years old. I believe that one of the reasons for his longevity, was he committed his life to making people laugh which in turn made himself laugh. During World War II, The Korean Conflict and the Vietnam War, he made numerous trips to the front lines with his famous USO Tours. His only objective was to lift the spirits and attitudes of our heroic soldiers with laughter. These young fighting men and women were facing tremendous horrors on a daily basis and just being able to laugh for a few hours probably made a huge difference in how each one of these brave souls faced the next day.

Laughter has always been a human necessity, not just an entertainment luxury. Even the kings of old had a court jester. You talk about a stressful job…His only job was to make the king laugh. The problem with being a comedian back then was, if you didn't make the king laugh, Oops, you didn't just get fired or a rotten tomato or egg thrown at you…it was Off with Your Head…! Life is full of issues and tribulations that we face on a daily basis. Every day we are confronting problems with our finances, employment, relationships, not to mention our health. When we make decisions concerning these issues, we MUST NOT let Fear come into play. Here is why. If you allow worry and fear to take over and dominate your thoughts, even simple things will become threatening. They can cloud and blind your common sense of reality and good judgement. So…STOP IT…! Quit dwelling on the Negative.

**The attitude you're in when you tackle these issues and problems,
Will determine the Level of Success you will have in Conquering Them…!
So, why not have a Positive One…?**

FEAR: Always becomes worse when you dwell on it. It will multiply into a full-blown mental catastrophe if you let it continue. Take this scenario for instance:

That pain in your side, it's probably nothing and you had too much to eat BUT – Negative thoughts will start attacking your common sense…O My, that's probably cancer…my mother had it, my grandmother had it too…It's probably my time to get it…! If you let it, the Fear WILL get worse…and you start thinking things like: I'll end up in the hospital taking chemotherapy and radiation treatment…what will I do about my kids and my dog??? AND the thoughts can get worse…I wonder what people will say at my Funeral…and on, and on, and on…!!!

The cure is simple, don't let your imagination run crazy toward the negative side of your thinking. Change your Attitude with positive thoughts, mental pictures and memories.

Here are some really factual and positive things that happen to your body when you laugh. Laughter releases a chemical called Endorphins in the brain. Which gives you a feeling of euphoria and happiness, this reduces stress and anxiety. Laughter can lower your blood pressure. It triggers the right side of the brain, which is the creative side. We all know that taking vitamin C and things like drinking green tea and eating an apple a day will help boost your immune system but guess what, laughing increases your body's production of antibodies and T-cells that fight off disease and will boost your immune system. Our first line of defense is our immune system. Did you know that studies have proven that laughter increased a body's tolerance to pain? So just consider when you are facing some painful health issues like arthritis, recovering from surgeries etc. laughing will help you get through some of the related pain that accompanies them. Think about this. According to research out of the University of Waterloo, people that have a strong sense of humor are less depressed and anxious than those with a less developed sense of humor.

We all know that stress is a real threat to a person's health. Like I have stated before, I do several Attitude Seminars at numerous

Assisted Living Homes for Seniors. During every one of these presentations, I use humor to keep the audience positive and focused. Every few minutes I will clown around and tell a humorous story or joke. The results are tremendous in how the audience will receive my information and retain it. Even some of the folks with Dementia and Alzheimer's have remembered me from past presentations.

I tell my audience to do some simple things to help change their attitudes from "Sad to Glad," I ask them if they remember the "I Love Lucy" show? They all say yes and I notice a grin will appear on their faces. Then I ask them if they remember when Lucy and Ethel were in the Chocolate Factory…and Voila…They all start laughing…! Amazing isn't it, that just mentioning the episode they changed their state of mind. I also ask them about Abbot and Costello's famous performance of "Who's on First?" They again will all nod their heads and get another huge smile on their faces. *(if you are younger and don't know about these shows or episodes – just look them up on YouTube and get ready to laugh…!)* If you are of a younger generation, choose one of your favorite current comedians' or shows that make you laugh and use them to induce some laughter into your attitude.

Whatever it takes to put a grin on your face and a change your attitude from one of stress and despair, make the effort and you will see an incredible change in your day. It will not only help you change your attitude but will affect everyone around you. Your spouse, kids, parents, friends and coworkers. (might even affect your Boss…LOL)

Feeling down and moody, watch one of your favorite movies or read one of your favorite books. Changing your attitude is NOT A PASSIVE ACTIVITY. Sometime it takes some real effort to take away all the anxiety and stress that today's society is placing upon us. I love to ask my audiences if they watch the news to raise their hands and 100% usually do. I then holler out real loud, "DON'T…" Just watching the daily news for five minutes can be detrimental to a persons' attitude and health.

Don't get me wrong. Please stay informed about what is going on in the world, just be selective on what you allow to affect your attitude. Today's news is mainly filled with sensationalism, which is usually of a Negative Nature. Whether it's about drive by shootings, rapes, muggings, fires, car accidents, foreign affairs or the never-ending issues about Politics and Religion. It will usually bring your attitude down. I know if the Television is on in the living room and its news time, I can't even walk through to the bedroom without hearing something that will either make me sad or angry. I have to put my "Attitude Protectors" into play and not let this influx of Negativity invade my brain and deplete my healthy attitude.

I tell people, It Ain't easy…! Somedays, we wake up and things just Ain't going right. This hurts and that don't feel good. You start worrying about finances, layoffs, relationships, the last checkup at the doctor's, in which the results were not favorable, along with so many other issues that we all can face. Well, all I can advise you to do is what I have said before and will say again and again:

"Change Your Attitude – Change Your Life"

At this very moment in time you have a crucial choice to make, and I hate to say it but YOU are the ONLY one who can successfully change your attitude. Other folks and things around you can help influence you but it will be up to you and the battle that goes on in your conscious mind that will determine the success or failure of the outcome. Getting into a positive state of mind and staying there is so important to your health. Ya gotta pull out all the stops and do whatever you have to do to achieve this positive state of mind.

Whenever you decide to use it, always keep in mind that laughter is a powerful tool for creating connections, lifting people up, and fighting life's toughest battles. When you hear laughter, you know that someone has made a choice to be happy, even if just for a moment. In troubling times, laughter can be courage in itself.

Aristotle said, "Laughter is bodily exercise, Precious to Health!"

"Hey Fred" you ask? "All this talk is really nice to hear, but HOW do you do it?" Well, in the following chapters, *(especially Chapter 8)* I will be addressing many principals and steps you can put into play that will help you change your attitude and not only get into a better mood but help to keep you there.

The main ingredient to successfully achieve all of the things that I will show you is simply this:

Your Willing Participation…!
So…!
Just Do It…!

You can actively participate in practicing these steps in creating a better attitude in your mind, heart and soul, Or Not…It is entirely up to you…! So, read on and I wish you fantastic success.

Time to Laugh

The Princess Frog

While I was strolling along the river bank in Dublin, there sitting by the babbling brook was a Huge Green Frog. Well, I was so excited and I reached down and picked it up before it could hop away. That frog looked me straight in the eye and spoke to me. She said in a high sweet voice, "If you give me a big kiss, I'll turn into a Beautiful Young Princess…!" I asked excitedly, "You mean, if I give you a big kiss you will turn into a Beautiful Young Princess…?" She said romantically, "YES…Now Give me a Big Kiss…!" To which I replied, "NO…!" Confused, she asked, "Don't you want me to turn into a Beautiful Young Princess…???" I politely told her, "Look Honey, I'm 75 years old…! **I'd rather have a Talking Frog…!!!**"

Attitude Thought #4

One Minute of Anger Weakens the Immune System for 4 to 5 Hours But One Minute of Laughter Boosts the Immune System for 24 Hours

Chapter Five

Why You Should Maintain a Positive Attitude

"Positive Thinking Will Not Let You to Do Everything,
But
It Will Let You to Do Everything Better Than Negative Thinking"
Zig Ziglar

Like Zig states in the opening quote, a positive attitude is not a cure all but it is such a necessary mind set to help everyone achieve and maintain such a higher level of success than having a negative attitude will. Since this book is about your health let me start off with a personal story of a health issue I experienced. I believe you will understand why I am such a firm believer in the importance of having a "Positive Unfailing Approach and Attitude Toward Your Health, Healing and Well Being."

I love telling this story because I get a chance to make you laugh, then to let you understand and realize the great results I experienced.

In 1989 I was working at a major semi-conductor company in Dallas, Texas. I noticed that my left ankle had developed an unusual pain. It really hurt, so I took two aspirin and the pain went away. However, about 5 hours later the pain returned. Hmm? So, I took two more aspirins and again the pain disappeared. Well, another 5 hours went by and the pain returned, so, I took another two aspirins. Being a relative intelligent human being (or so I thought) I repeated this again and again for almost a month. Unfortunately, I started getting this really bad pain in my lower left side in my stomach. I figured that another two aspirins were not going to fix this, so I went to see my doctor. He checked me over and told me that to really find out what was wrong, I needed to check into the hospital and have some tests and x-rays taken. Here is the fun part.

I gotta tell you folks, I have never been in the hospital before in my life and I came to an astonishing realization about one interesting issue.

I did not know
That I could get that
INTIMATE
With so many people
That I have NEVER met before in my Life…!

They do not care about your privacy. They put that silly hospital gown on you with those tiny string ties in the back, which leaves your 'Shining Integrity' exposed to everyone around! It becomes a little embarrassing…to say the least. I think they do it on purpose LOL…!

Every afternoon an orderly would come in with a clipboard and asked me to check off the items that I wanted for breakfast. Well, of course I checked off eggs, bacon, toast and you cannot do without coffee. So, I checked off coffee as well. I want you to know that Not Once, did I ever check off Apple Juice. Ya wanna know what I got every morning with my breakfast…? Yep, you guessed it, Apple Juice. @#$%^&. However, being a good patient, I would drink it. Well, one morning I just put the little container of Apple Juice in the drawer by my bed.

NOW - I have a question to ask all the nurse's out there.

Why do you all come in and ask, "How are 'WE' feeling…?" I'm laying here in bed and you are out and about and I'm probably not feeling as good as them. One day the nurse got really personal and said "It's time for 'OUR' urine sample." She handed me the little plastic cup and told me to call her when I was finished, she closed the curtain and left. Hmm…! I looked at the little plastic cup and thought about it for only one second and then, with a grin on my face, reached over and retrieved my saved Apple Juice from the drawer. Ya wanna guess what I did with that Apple Juice…Yep, you KNOW what I did…! I poured that Apple Juice right into that little cup and said in a loud voice, "We're Finished" She came back, opened the curtain and took the small cup from me. She held it up to the light and stated in a confused voice, "My goodness, we're looking a little cloudy today…!" to which I replied, "Really? Let me see that." She handed me the cup and as I looked at it with a puzzled look on my face, I exclaimed, "O My, it is a little cloudy, Let's pass it through one more time…!!!!" I drank it down and SHE FAINTED…!

They have not asked me back since…!

Now I will move on to the serious side of this conversation. After all the tests were performed, my doctor told me the pain I have been experiencing in my side was a Duodenal Ulcer. He said that I needed to quit taking the aspirin because it was eating away at the lining in my stomach and was what had caused the ulcer. He then smiled and said the good news is, we can repair it with some prescription medication. Whew…! I was a happy camper and really relieved to hear that news. So, I quit taking the aspirin and started taking the prescription medication.

However, two days later something happened to my body that I DID NOT LIKE…! When I woke up, every bone, every joint, every muscle in my entire body Hurt So Bad…I had never felt that kind of intense pain in my entire life. It felt like a huge truck had just ran over me. When I moved my finger it hurt, if I blinked my eye it hurt. I was truly frightened and scared at what was happening. I called my doctor and he had me check myself back into the hospital to have some more tests run. After the test were taken and evaluated my doctor sat me down and told me the results. He said I had an extremely serious case of **Debilitating Rheumatoid Arthritis (DRA).** He told me that the aspirin I had been taking was a non-steroidal anti-inflammatory drug (NSAID) and had helped repress the onslaught of my arthritis. Then with a solemn voice he dropped a bombshell on me…He said that my condition was extremely serious and in a few years it would deteriorate and disfigure my bones and joints enough that I would lose a lot of mobility in my hands and probably need to have my hip joints replaced, as well as a few others. OUCH...! That was not an outcome I wanted to hear or experience.

As a reader of this book, so far, I have been preaching to you the **Absolute Necessity of having a Positive Attitude and saying things Out Loud**. Well, here is where I took a stand and looked that doctor straight in the eye and told him in no uncertain terms:

**NO IT WON'T
I will not let this Arthritis Control Me,
I WILL CONTROL IT...!**

That was in 1989, it is now 31 years later, I am 75 years old and because of the care of a good conscientious Doctor and My God Given Positive Attitude...I have maintained really stable Joint health. I have had no joint replacements, I am very active, busy and mobile. I walk, exercise, present seminars, and do speaking engagements and singing concerts.

Several Doctors and professionals that I have discussed my case with were impressed with the lack of more joint deformity that usually accompanies folks with DRA. Especially at my age and for this length of time. Here is what I want you to take to heart:

I have been told by many professionals that My <u>Positive Attitude</u> and My willingness to follow thru with their instructions have played a MAJOR part in my Healing Longevity.

Please understand, I don't want you to start getting the idea that having a positive attitude is a cure all miracle answer to all your health issues. I DO want you to understand, that your attitude plays such a critical part of your healing and recovery of the health issues that you experience.

Many people with health issues tell me, "But, you don't understand how bad it hurts or how it makes me feel." I will tell you up front..." Oh YES I DO know exactly what they mean and I know what they feel...!" Here's why I say this.

I did not say that my Debilitating Rheumatoid Arthritis has gone away, I just said it was NOT going to Control Me or my life. It still rears its ugly head from time to time. I have had some serious swelling and aching joints that have almost immobilized my arm, wrist, ankle, etc. This is when my attitude toward this stupid disease comes into play. I will immediately begin to verbally assault whatever area that is affected by saying out loud "Positive Affirmations" (I will address these in a later chapter.) If my wrist is affected, I will focus on it by touching the area and saying things like, "This swelling will not last and will go away…I will not allow this pain to disable me…. My body will reject this pain and swelling…etc." I also try to think of ways to make myself laugh and change my mood. This approach to any illness or issue that a person has will begin to change the chemistry in their body by releasing endorphins and your body's production of antibodies and T-cells that fight off disease and will reinforce their immune system, which will help repress and reduce the pain, swelling and other conditions you are feeling.

Our bodies have incredible healing processes that are already inherent in our DNA. Take this example for instance. Have you ever had a broken bone or know someone that did? I bet you have. The process goes like this: The doctor will set the bone, then put it in a cast to immobilize the area…Then what does the doctor do next? Nothing, they just smile and send you home to collect autographs on your cast…! He does not heal the bone with treatment or medication…but somehow the bone will knit itself together and become strong once again…Hmmm…!!! Amazing, isn't it? If you have had a simple cut on your skin and basically clean and bandage it, what happens to that cut? Yep, in a week or so it begins to heal and the skin will renew itself and most of the time will not even leave a scar. Once again, I say, Hmmm…? I often ask my audiences if they ever rode a bicycle or got on roller skates, to which they all reply with a resounding 'Yes.' I also ask them if they ever fell off and skinned their knees…to which they all laugh and say "Yes" again. I tell them that my mother used to put those "Iron on Patches" on my blue jeans 4 deep because I kept skinning my knees. I had scabs on scabs, but Ya know what? I do not have any scars on my knees and you probably don't either. This should reinforce the fact in your mind that if you work in conjunction with your mind and body, you can help amplify the natural healing process that you already have that is inherent in your own body.

Have any of you heard the term **"Placebo Effect or Placebo Response?"** If you have great and it's not a problem if you haven't. The Oxford Dictionary defines a "Placebo" as: *a harmless pill, medicine or procedure prescribed more for the psychological benefit to the patient, than for any Physiological effect.*

Here is another fact: The word 'Placebo' is a Latin term meaning "I shall be pleasing" so it means something good…!

Some of you might remember the actor *Johnny Wiessmuller* who played the *Edgar Rice Burroughs* character *'Tarzan'* in the 1930's and 40's movies. If not, and you are younger you will have at least seen some remake of *'Tarzan'* in one form or another. You might want to ask me, "Fred? Why are you bringing up old *'Tarzan'* movies when we are talking about placebos?" Well, that's a fair question and I want you to allow me to paint a picture in your mind, as the answer.

In so many of these movies there was usually a unique character in the native tribes known as the "Medicine Man" and in my eyes, was always a very strange individual. He usually wore a big animal skin coat with some kind of animal headgear with horns coming out of it and usually had a bone through his nose. This guy usually had more necklaces than *Mr. T* did, except the Medicine Mans necklace and bracelets were made out of old teeth-n-bones and not gold. I always thought this guy was more of a comic relief and not an important figure in the tribe. I mean, if someone was sick in the tribe, they would bring this Medicine Man in to take care of him. Now I really want you to try and visualize the picture I want to paint in your head…!

This odd character wearing the horned headdress, furry robe and jewelry made out of teeth would mix some herbs and liquid goop to give the patient to drink, and then begin to rattle some bones over the body with one hand while swinging a dead

chicken over his head with the other and chanting some odd group of gibberish in the attempts to cure this ill native.

At the time, I thought this was really dumb and goofy. Not only that but it was really hard to keep from laughing. However, as I began to study this Medicine Man phenomenon, my education began to broaden. For one, I found out that the Medicine Man in most tribes (including our Native American Indian Tribes) was usually more powerful than the actual chief of the tribe. Hmmmm…! He commanded a position of high respect and honor to all the members of the tribe. As I dug deeper, I began to see the reason he commanded this type of respect. I could see how a native that was stricken with a fever or sickness, laying on a makeshift bed shivering with this illness and wanting only one thing…which would be…TO GET WELL…! Now to this native, the Medicine Man does not look goofy or dumb…he looks powerful and connected to the gods of the tribe and has the magical ability to make him well. So, as this Powerful Medicine Man chants, swings the chicken over his head, rattles the bones…this ill native BELIEVES that all the Spirits of this Evil Sickness are being driven from his body.

Before I continue with the "Tarzan" scenario, let me explain some research results of the "Placebo Effect"

Research on the placebo effect has focused on the relationship of <u>mind and body</u>. One of the most common theories is that the placebo effect is due to a person's expectations. If a person expects a pill to do something, then it's possible that the <u>body's own chemistry</u> can cause effects similar to what a medication might have caused.

In a nutshell, a person given such an ineffectual treatment will often have a perceived or actual improvement in their condition. So, instead of giving the ill native a pill as the placebo…the chanting and bone rattling becomes the placebo, thus pointing to the importance of <u>Perception</u> and The Brains Role in Physical Health. This native believes that he is being healed by the most powerful and honorable man and leads us to this famous quote:

"AS A MAN THINKETH"

I guess you could say to the native that was ill, the Placebo Medicine Man "Changed His Attitude and Changed His Health"

So, if you are ever ill, just call me and I will come over to your house, swing a chicken over your head and chant some gibberish…My rates are Cheap, Cheap Cheap…!!!

With all that was said above, can I ask each of you one simple question? Why would you not do everything you can possibly do, to help your own body, fight and control the health issues that you are faced with by simply changing your attitude???

Time to Laugh

That's When the Fight Started

Me and the Misses were out shopping at our local grocery store. As I pushed the cart down one aisle, I noticed a sign that said in big bold letters: **24 Cans of Beer for $20…!** Wow, I thought that was a great deal and immediately reached down and picked up the case of beer and placed it in the cart. My wife gave me a really condescending look and hastily took the case of beer out of the cart and put it back on the shelf. Stunned I asked her, "Why did you do that Love?" She said, "That's too expensive." Well, saddened but not wanting to argue, I went along with her decision. We continued through the store and turned down the aisle where all the make-up is located. My wife quickly picked up a jar of face cream and placed it in the cart. I was really amazed and said, "Hey, that cost $40.00." She smiled and said, "I know but it makes me beautiful." To my defense I boldly replied, "So will 24 cans of Beer and there $20 dollars Cheaper…!"   **THAT'S WHEN THE FIGHT STARTED…!**

Attitude Thought #5

| If You work in conjunction with Your mind and body, by having a Better Attitude, You will help Amplify the Natural Healing process Already inherent within Your own body |

Chapter Six

Good Thoughts and Actions

*"Anxiety Does Not Empty Tomorrow of Its Sorrow
But
Only Empties Today of Its Strength"*
Charles Spurgeon

I would like you to consider a statement from a book *"As A Man Thinketh"* written and by **James Allen**. It was published in 1902 and the contents and advice are still applicable to today's issues.

He stated, *"**Good thoughts and actions** can never produce bad results; Bad thoughts and actions can never produce good results. This is but saying that nothing can come from corn but corn, nothing from nettles but nettles. Men understand this law in the natural world, and work with it; but few understand it in the mental and moral world (though its operation there is just as simple and undeviating), and they, therefore, do not cooperate with it."*

Throughout time we have always had things that influence our thinking. However, today we are bombarded with an overflow of information from, TV, Magazines, News, Movies, Books and do I even need to mention the added effect of Cell Phones and the INTERNET? With all this great technology we are more connected and totally informed than ever before. The problem is that so much of this vast amount of input is NEGATIVE. God Forbid the NEWS would sensationalize something Positive in their daily reports. NOPE, they focus mostly on the Gloom and Doom and they will inform you of it, beginning with the Morning News at 6, 8 and 9 AM News. Then if that doesn't infiltrate your mind enough, they will bombard you again with the 4:00 O-Clock News, then remind you at 5 O-Clock & 6 O-Clock. But Wait…to top it all off they will hit you one more time, right before you go to bed, with the 10:00 O-Clock News…! Holy Smokes, it's a wonder we don't all have nightmares every night.

When we allow our minds to be constantly contaminated with these negative thoughts our thinking becomes effected and distorted. Our attitudes are filled with anxiety, stress, worry and fear. These begin to wear us down and affect, not only your life, but everyone around you. Your spouse, children, parents, friends, co-workers, etc.

I want you to consider a very real and present example of this process that is going on as I am writing this book. At the beginning of 2020 the Entire World was blindsided with a new Coronavirus called COVID-19. Overnight it became a Global Pandemic and turned the world upside down. It has been frightening and scary enough just going through the "Stay in Place" orders, businesses having to shut down, schools closing and so many negative things as a result of it. It has been a challenge for every human being on this planet. Every day we are glued to our TV's just to keep up with all the Daily Events that are surrounding this "Silent Killer." Don't get me wrong because I want all of you to stay informed and we all want to know what is going on and what we need to do to stay Safe, Protected and Healthy. We also want to know what our leaders in government are doing and where we stand. This is all natural and we all want to be informed and up to date. However, and I say this in respect to everyone reading this and going through this horrible ordeal.

It is Extremely Critical
That You Have and Maintain a
Positive Attitude

Now I know you are going to ask me, "How the heck do you accomplish this impossible feat?" When every day we are given the devasting numbers of how many new cases of this virus have been found along with the ever-rising death toll. Every news cast contains nothing but Negative News about this disease. Even some of the commercials have a negative tone to them. Not only that but both political parties are bickering, arguing and pointing fingers. Whew…! I will admit that it is extremely scary and it will tear at our emotions. However, now is where the fact that by now, you understand and know ---

YOU DO HAVE A CHOICE

The things that are happening are happening regardless of whether we like it or not. We can only effect things that we are personally in control of. Things like how we spend our time, our money, our relationships, what we eat, wear, exercise and so on and so on. The choice we all have when we approach these issues is really simple. However, when it comes to our attitude it becomes a bit more complicated.

I would like to insert a fantastic statement about the *"Importance of Attitude"* by *Charles R. Swindoll*

"The longer I live, the more I realize the impact of attitude on life. Attitude, to me, is more important than facts. It is more important than the past, the education, the money, than circumstances, than failure, than successes, than what other people think or say or do. It is more important than appearance, giftedness or skill. It will make or break a company... a church... a home. The remarkable thing is we have a choice everyday regarding the attitude we will embrace for that day. We cannot change our past... we cannot change the fact that people will act in a certain way. We cannot change the inevitable. The only thing we can do is play on the one string we have, and that is our attitude. **I am convinced that life is 10% what happens to me and 90% of how I react to it.** *And so, it is with you...* **We are in charge of our Attitudes.**"

This simple statement about 10% vs 90% created a monumental change in the way I approach EVERY issue that crosses my path. It doesn't matter if it is something good or bad, the first thing I say out loud is "Well that's the 10%" which sets my mind and attitude on a positive approach to what and how I will handle and react with the remaining 90%. Just by slowing down and thinking about this gives me an incredible advantage over the usual panic reaction of "O My

God…What am I going to do now…???" It helps to chase the fear and anxiety out of the issue, no matter what it is.

So, whatever the 10% issues you are faced with…you can either let all these issues begin to depress and destroy you with a Negative Attitude, or you can climb above them and react to them by choosing to have a 90% winning Positive Attitude. You can either be victorious or you can become a victim. You gotta get prepared each and every day, to do battle with your attitude. You can either prepare for victory or you can set yourself up for defeat. Like I said before, having a Positive Attitude, is not a Passive Activity. It takes some hard decisions and hard discipline to fight all the negative issues. HOWEVER --- The choice you make, positive or negative, will have a definite effect on your Health. So, again I ask, "How important is your Health to You and the people around you….?"

In short we need to quit dwelling on what is wrong, seeing all the faults and instead, find the silver lining in each dark cloud…if you don't you will be in the manufacturing business…and the product you manufacture will not only be sadness and unhappiness but absolutely and totally **Bad for Your Health**. Worry, like faith, is a spiritual force. Like a magnet, it attracts the very things we fear, clouds our judgment and distorts our perspective. God never intended us to carry tomorrow's burdens along with todays.

"Do not be anxious about tomorrow" Matthew 6:34

Did you know:
1. 40% of the things we worry about never happen.
2. 30% have already happened and we can't do anything about them.
3. 22% are needless worries about health, finances, relationships, etc.
4. 4% are things real things we can't do something about.
5. 4% are things real things we can do something about.

So, all the things we read, listen to, watch and absorb will have an effect on our health. Thus, going back to the beginning statement of this chapter "Good Thoughts and Actions" it really makes sense, that if our input is as positive and uplifting as we can possibly make it, the results and outcome will be far better than if we allow all the negative and depressing thoughts invade our thinking…! It's your choice and you can either plant and produce Corn or Nettles / Positives or Negatives, because it's a law in the natural world.

Time to Laugh

4 Weeks to Live

Three of us blokes were having a friendly chat with Father O'Malley after the church service and he asked us one simple question; "What would you do if you only had 4 weeks left to live?" O'Leary was the first to speak up and said, "Well, I would go home and spend as much time with my wife and kids, just loving on them and being with them till the end…! Father said, "That's wonderful" Then O'Hara spoke up and said, "Myself, I would volunteer for everything at the church to help as many people that I could." To which Father O'Malley replied, "That's commendable" That's when Father O'Malley turned to me and asked, "Freddy, what would you do?" I smiled and answered him, "I would spend the last 4 weeks of my life with me Mother-In-Law…!" With a look of surprise on his face Father O'Malley asked, "Freddy, why in the world would you want to do that?" "Well Father." I said, **'That would be the Longest 4 weeks of My Life…!!!"**

Attitude Thought #6

> I am convinced that
> Life is 10% of what happens to You
> And
> 90% of how You React to It

Chapter Seven

The Power of Positive Affirmations
"Self-Talk" & Building Your Self-Esteem

"Staying positive does not mean you have to be happy all the time
It just means that even on Hard Days
you know there are better ones coming"

    If you are like 99.999% of the entire population, you talk to yourself. Yep, we do it when we're alone. We talk to ourselves as we get dressed in the morning looking in the mirror, driving to and from work, (this does not include what we politely say out loud to the other drivers.) We do this when we are out in the yard mowing the grass, in the shower, washing the dishes, doing laundry and so on and so on.

    This is natural, However, have you ever listened to HOW you talk to yourself? I think you'd be surprised at some of the things you say in private to yourself during the course of a day. We, as humans, tend to be a little critical, especially of ourselves. We also tend to verbalize the negative and not the positive side of things. Have you ever caught yourself saying things like?

1. I'll never be able to lose this weight.
2. I'm sure I won't be able to pass this test.
3. I never get a raise or promotion.
4. Why can't I ever do anything right?
5. I'll never be able to quit this addiction.
   Or one of the worst…
6. I don't think I'll ever - (Fill in the Blank with 'Get Well' 'Get out of Debt' 'Be Happy' and so many other issues)

    The list could go on and on and on. These little bits of criticism are known as Negative Affirmations and if we say them, or things like them, to ourselves every day, they will have a drastic effect on our Attitude, our Success and definitely our Health. In the past chapters I have presented several examples to show you why you need to stay away from a lot of the daily negative issues that invade our minds.

In this chapter I want to really expand on the importance of Self-Talk and Positive Affirmations…here's why;

**Self-Talk is One of the most powerful means of Communication
Because it can either
Empower You or Defeat You**

Here is a short definition of what an Affirmation is:

A short phrase that you repeat to yourself at least once a day

The reason these affirmations are so powerful is simply because they are entirely personal and are a verbal identification of what we think of ourselves. These thoughts can be either positive or negative and this my friend, is where you have the opportunity to make an extremely important decision…! These short phrases that we repeat over and over again will have an unbelievable effect on our Self-Esteem. Our Self-Esteem is how we view ourselves and as human beings, each of us, inherently have a need to be recognized, have a sense of value and respect. When we are depressed and stressed out it is so easy to fall into the mental trap of negative self-talk. "I knew this would happen…I'll never get better!" – "This treatment isn't doing me any good!" – "My grandmother had something like this and never got better!" – and Bla, Bla, Bla, Bla…Until you have deteriorated your attitude, imbalanced your immune system, and consequently your Health…! Your body has a hard time trying to stay in a healing mode when you mind keeps telling your body to "FORGET IT…IT WON'T WORK…!" So, like I have said before and will repeat again and again.

"Change Your Attitude – Change Your Health"

Self-esteem is basically the foundation of how we picture ourselves and who we are. If you think back to your childhood, try to remember some of the things that your parents and people around you said as you were growing up. We all have seen the results to kids that grew up under continued negative statements and positive statements.

If a child grew up in a negative atmosphere with statements like:
1. You're so clumsy, you would trip on a blade of grass.
2. Why do you do stupid things?
3. Why can't you be more like so and so?
4. Don't be a baby.
5. Why can't you do anything right?
6. You're so Lazy.

Well, you get the picture and you also know that this type of rhetoric, when said to a child over and over, will have a dramatic and negative effect on that child's self-esteem.

However, on the other hand if that child grew up in a positive atmosphere with statements like:

1. You are a really smart kid.
2. You can do anything you put your mind to.
3. I knew you could do it.
4. You are really doing better.
5. All of us make mistakes
6. You make me smile.

Wow…! What a difference these statements would make in that child's self-esteem.

So, it makes sense that the things we heard as a child, either positive or negative, helped shape our Self-Esteem and who we are today. We cannot go back and change the past BUT consequently and more importantly the things we say out loud to ourselves today, either positive or negative,
WILL Shape Our Self-Esteem
and

Who We Will Become Tomorrow

Stress & Low Self Esteem takes a toll on our mental health and thus a nasty toll on our physical health. Negative self-talk is linked to chronic stress and is the main culprit for a host of diseases, addiction included. Studies have shown how repressed anger can lead to hypertension, cardiovascular disease, digestive disorders and infection,

I hope the above paragraphs have painted a grim and truthful picture of how dangerous and damaging these subliminal messages of negative self-talk and affirmations can be to our total wellbeing and our overall health.

NOW...!

Let's make a 180-degree change in direction and focus on the POSITIVE benefits of Self-Talk and Positive Affirmations and the Tremendous Positive Effect that they will have on every person, and I mean every person, that will participate in using them.

Many leading psychologists in recent years has revealed the numerous health benefits of positive affirmations, such as better sleep, a stronger immune system, faster recovery from illness, less stress with better health and a longer life expectancy. Earlier in chapter 2, I told you about the Oncologists I interviewed and what they said about how beneficial a positive attitude toward their cancer patient's recovery.

The patient's attitude is so paramount and plays such a vital role in their approach to treatment. The ones that have a Strong Positive Attitude and a Will to Fight, usually recover Faster, Quicker and More Completely than those with a Negative Attitude.

This is how strong and valuable having a Positive Attitude and Having a daily Positive Self-Talk conversation with yourself can be towards a Healthier and Happier Life.

Illness and Diseases are NOT a Respecter a Persons
Age
Gender
Race
Color
Creed
Religion
Or Even the Type of Music You Like

Illness and Disease can strike anyone at any time. Remember earlier I told you about my experience with Debilitating Rheumatoid Arthritis…I was 44 years old, healthy, trim, not overweight, active, I exercised and overall, I was in really good shape. But out of the blue this disease hit me like a ton of bricks. Don't know why, but it did and that stupid arthritis did not care one iota about who or what I was. In other words, we never know when we might be blind sighted with a health issue. My question to you is;

If an Illness or Disease Happens to YOU
What Are YOU going to DO…?

I am sure the first thing you will do is to go see your doctor and follow his/her advice and their recommendations. If they prescribe a prescription with rest, do it. If they feel you need to diet and exercise, do it. If they feel you need surgery, do it. If they feel you need Chemotherapy and Radiation treatments, do it. You will probably follow these recommendations to the letter and hope that this will lead you down the road of making you healthy and healed again. But you can't stop there because there is so much more that you can do that will make all these recommendations and treatments more affective in the healing process. So, don't just wring your hands and say "O Well, I'll just have to live with it." You need to establish an unquestionable positive attitude in your heart and soul that you are going to;

"Do Every Thing That You Can Possibly Do!"

"Okay Fred," you ask me, "What else can I do…?"

During World War II, Winston Churchill gave his famous speech called the "Never Give Up…!" speech. He stood up at the podium and said, "Never Give In, Never Give In, Never, Never, Never, Never, Never…(I don't know how many times he repeated 'Never' but he said it over and over again) Never, Never, Never Give in…IN NOTHING…!!!" This is the attitude you need to say to yourself, concerning whatever your health issues might be. Wither it's about a common cold or stage 4 Cancer…Fight it and NEVER, NEVER, NEVER…GIVE IN…!

So, you can **Never Give In** by using everything at your disposal to stay as Positive as you can. And I know that some days THAT AIN'T EASY. Ya wake up and your shoulder hurts, your Blood Pressure is way out of whack, you have a Radiation Treatment scheduled for today, your Medical Report tells you that you have a serious Health Issue, I could make a list of negative things that could affect you that would reach the moon. The following Chapter will consist of some of the things that you can do to achieve the best attitude each day, regardless of all the CRAP that invades your mind.

Time to Laugh

The Inspection Tour

After knocking on the door, Mrs. O'Leary opened it and looked at me with a puzzled expression. "Freddy…?" She asked, "Where is Mr. O'Leary? He went to the Brewery with Ya for the Inspection Tour?" Sadly, I told her, "Well, Mrs. O'Leary, I have some very bad news for Ya. While we were at the Brewery doing the Inspections. Mr. O'Leary fell into a huge Vat of Beer and Drowned…!" "O Good Gracious…!" She cried out in total disdain. "Me husband fell into a vat of beer and drowned…!" She fell down and cried and cried. After a while she finally composed herself, looked up at me with tears flowing from her eyes and asked, "Tell me one thing Freddy…Did he go Quickly…?" I tenderly held her hand and replied. **"NO…He Climbed out 3 Times to PEE…!!!!"**

Attitude Thought #7

**Self-Talk is One of the most powerful means of Communication
Because it can either
Empower You or Defeat You**

Chapter Eight

How to Achieve the Best Positive Attitude Possible And Hold on to it Through Out the Entire Day

"Staying positive does not mean you are happy all the time
It just means that even on the Hard Days
You know You Always
HAVE A CHOICE"

Staying as healthy as possible is a goal that we all want to achieve. It's nice to have a list of things or steps you can take to get into, and stay in, that Healthy Positive State of Mind that will help you combat all the negative vibes that are thrown at us on a daily basis. Well, this is the chapter that will help guide you through so many ways that you can, not only fight the negativity but be Victorious over it. We just covered the fantastic advantages of Self-Talk and Positive Affirmations…. So……Let's continue with……………!

MAKE A LIST

One very essential thing, is to make a list of Positive Affirmations that FIT your specific needs. You can actually call them **"Recovery Affirmations"** For instance, if you are battling Diabetes list all the ways that you can positively affect, not just the recommendations your medical professional has given you, but things that you can say to keep your mind and body functioning in a Fight to the Finish Winning Mode.

The obvious things are of course;
1. I **will** watch my weight.
2. I **will** exercise today.
3. I **will** measure my insulin levels.
4. I **will** get a good night's sleep.

Now, why not add these Recovery Affirmations to your list, things like;
5. Every day my Body **is** defeating this Diabetes.
6. Every day my blood sugar and blood pressure levels **are** becoming increasingly stable.
7. Every day **I am** able to manage my Stress Levels.
8. Every day **is** a journey to enjoy.
9. I **Will** make myself Laugh Today.
10. I **Will** overcome this illness.
11. I **Will** be Grateful for this Day.
12. Every time I take this medicine it **IS Helping** my body get healthier.

Did you notice the Bold printed and underlined words…I did this so that you will understand the importance that it's;

**Not Only What You Say
But
How You Say It…!**

When you repeat these Recovery Affirmations out loud to yourself every day and sometimes, many times a day, with a strong resolve in your voice, your mind and body begin to work in harmony with the treatments that your doctor has prescribed for you. So, tailor your list towards whatever health issue you are personally faced with.

Take any illness or disease you can think of and the same principles will apply. When I get an Arthritic Flare up in my joints (see chapter 5) I immediately start saying these types of Recovery Affirmations again and again. This helps to focus my mind and body on the area affected. Does it hurt? Darn right it hurts, but as I repeat these types of affirmations, my worry, goes away, my stress goes down, my heart rate becomes normal, and the FEAR of the Flare Up is taken away. This allows my immune system to work at its fullest and help to naturally deflate this flair up and the pain associated with it.

So, like I said, MAKE A LIST.

NO…! NOT LATER…!
STOP
Right Now,
Get a piece of paper a pen and
MAKE A LIST…!

You know the issues you are facing, so start a list now…! Make it simple for now, you can always add to it or change it later. This way you will have some Healing Affirmations to say out loud before you go to bed tonight and the first thing you will be able to say in the morning, when you look at that shinning face in the mirror.

Here are some generic examples that you should say every day to get you started. You need to say these statements, REGARDLESS of what kind of day it is or how you actually feel. Saying these statements out loud will help guide you into a positive mindset and not allow you to focus on negative or toxic thoughts.

1. This is going to be a Beautiful Day!
2. I will be happy and enjoy this entire day!
3. I choose to be Happy on Purpose!
4. I will not allow anyone to Steal My Joy Today!
5. I will not allow Setbacks to Discourage Me

Now---Start adding whatever Positive Affirmations that will fit your specific needs…!

Make yourself a promise that you will read this list out loud, at least, once first thing in the morning and once before you go to bed. Even when things are the darkest, please make that commitment to yourself. Remember, this is not a Passive Activity. You have to do it even when you don't feel like it or want to.

MAKE YOUR SELF LAUGH

Remember in Chapter 4 about Laughter being the Best Medicine. Well it is so beneficial to our wellbeing and it is sad that too many people go through life in a grumpy and unhappy mood. If you want to help defeat any of the health issues that you are facing, then it is IMPEARITIVE that you are NOT one of these Gloom and Doom Creatures that spread Negativity around like melted butter.

If you want to help promote your immune system and allow healing endorphins course though your body, then;

Ya Gotta Laugh
And
Ya Gotta Laugh a Lot

Think of who your favorite comedians are and google them on the internet. I promise you there will be hundreds of YouTube videos that you can watch for free. You can spend hours watching, Red Skelton, Bob Hope, Richard Prior, Jack Benny, Abbott and Costello, and so many new ones that are coming out. If you are not able to get on the internet, some of their CD's and tapes are available to order.

Watch some of your favorite movies or read funny books and magazines that make you laugh. Do whatever you can to get and keep a smile on your face. I promise you that it will help your health and your way to recovery.

I told you before that Changing Your Attitude is not a Passive Activity. You can't just sit there and wait for something or someone to come along and make you laugh. You have to actively find the things that tickle your funny bone and use them daily.

Surround Yourself with Positive People

Remember when we talked about asking someone the "How are you Feeling Today…?" question…? And they unloaded all their woes and miseries on you. You cannot spend all your time with negative people and you need to politely get away from them as quickly as you can. If most of your friends are always complaining, whining and groaning…they will always try to drag you down into the same pits of despair they live in. This is so damaging to your Health and Wellbeing. Don't get me wrong, I am not trying to tell you that you need to drop all your longtime friends that lean toward the negative side. What I am trying to suggest is that you consider adding some new relationships with a group of folks that will Encourage, Inspire and Motivate you. If you look for them you will find them and you will be so much better off if you do. Spending time with them will help balance out the negative input from the 'Nay Sayers'. If you cannot physically go out and meet new folks, then I suggest you invest in some CD's/Tapes of some good Motivational Speakers like: Zig Ziglar, Tony Robbins, Les Brown to name a few. Listening to them will inspire and encourage you while building up your self-esteem. If you are on the internet, just google any of them or 'Positive Mental Attitude' and you will be overwhelmed with information.

Focus on the Good Things

I know that we all have experienced lying in bed at night and Wham...out of nowhere your mind is filled with all the past mistakes and you made...either yesterday or in your dim past. Financial worries creep into your thoughts and health issues plague your mind. Please do not fall into that trap and dwell on them. One simple thing I like to use is the analogy of "Changing the Channel on Your TV." I remember when TV's came out and dad brought home our first one. I was about 9 years old and we were so excited just watching the old Indian Chief test pattern. Remember, back then to change the channel, you had to physically get up walk over to the TV set and turn the channel tuner. My dad was lucky, he had a remote back then...You say no way --- Yes, he did...It was ME. I can still hear him saying, "Son, get up and go change the channel, and don't turn it to fast!" Today, thank God, we have real remotes because there are a gazillion channels to change to...Back then we only had 3...!

When these Toxic Thoughts begin to invade your mind it's like watching a very bad or scary movie. Remember you are in control and you have the remote. It is a great mental exercise to picture yourself, pointing that remote at those negative thoughts and changing the channel to some good memories and happy thoughts. Don't give your imagination a chance to run crazy toward the negative side of your thinking. No one is immune to these invasive and negative intrusions, including myself. When I sense these negative thoughts beginning to take root in my mind, I reach up and physically turn the imaginary dial to a different station. In my mind, those stations will be anything from cartoons, the last steak dinner I had, my grandkids…in other words anything pleasant that will defeat and blot out the Evil Channel. Every time I do this, it always puts a smile on my face. Try it, I promise you it will work.

Change Your Got To's into Your Get To's

Have you ever found yourself really getting tired of hearing folks (including yourself) always saying – I GOT TO do this, I GOT TO do that, with just about everything they do. That phrase in itself has a hidden depressing and negative meaning to it. It's like saying "O woe is me, I GOT TO do this and that." Which has an unpleasant ring to it. Take these statements for instance;

I Got To go to work today.
I Got To drive in this traffic.
I Got To vacuum the house.
I Got To fix dinner.
I Got To walk the dog.
I Got To go to school.

They all sound like a difficult and unlikeable task that we GOT TO go do. Well, I have some good news for you. The way to change that is so simple.

Instead of saying it with the "I GOT TO" statement say;

I am so fortunate to have a JOB – Today I GET TO go to work!
I am so fortunate to own a Car - So I GET TO drive in this traffic!
I am so fortunate to own a Home – I GET TO Vacuum!
I am so fortunate to have Food in the refrigerator – I GET TO fix Dinner!

I am so fortunate to have a loyal and loving Dog – I GET TO take him for a walk!

I am so fortunate to have access to gain knowledge – I GET TO go to school!

See, the difference…even though it's very subtle, it will change the way you look at all the things you have to accomplish and do every day. It is amazing how your mind will process this in a positive manner instead of creating a negative twist to whatever you need to go do. This my friend is good for your attitude and consequently your health.

The same rule applies to how you use the phrase "I AM" in a sentence. These two words are extremely powerful and can guide your mindset into a Healthy Positive Attitude or a Devastating Negative Attitude. The trick is to be careful of the word you use directly after these two words. As an example, if you are always saying things like:

I AM (never) going to lose weight.
I AM (never) going to get well.
I AM (never) going to break this habit.

As you can already see, these statements and the way you say them, can begin to mentally defeat your desire to lose weight, get well, break a habit or whatever. So, why not take the word (Never) out of the equation or add things like:

I AM (on my way) to losing weight!
I AM (on my way) to getting well!
I AM (on my way) to breaking this habit!

You get the picture…The words you use to describe your situation or what you're going to do about it, are so important as to how your mind will process them and cause your body to react to them. You can either inhibit your immune system or boost it…You Have a Choice. I like this quote from *Tony Robbins*;

Our lives aren't shaped by our conditions.

Our lives are shaped by our decisions.
And the most important decision is where to direct your focus.
If your mind is undirected,
It will always look for what's wrong,
And you will be filled with
Stress and Anxiety

So, Decide to Focus on the **Right Things to Say** and the **Right Way to Say Them**.
The choice is yours and yours alone.
1. Make a List.
2. Make Yourself Laugh.
3. Surround Yourself with Positive People.
4. Focus on the Good Things.
5. Change Your Got To's into Your GET To's.

Time to Laugh

The Irish Divorce

I was sitting at home in Texas when the phone rang. I picked it up and it was my Irish Father in Dublin, Ireland. He said to me, "Freddy, I have to tell you something you're not going to like." He continued, "Your mother and I have been married for over 50 years and we are so sick and tired of each other that we have decided to get a divorce…!" "WHAT…!" I exclaimed, "Father Ya can't do that…!" "O Yes we can, Freddy." He answered, "We can't stand one another, we're getting a divorce, and that's final." Then he added, "Call your sister and tell her what are plans are." And he hung up…! Well, I immediately called my sister and told her the terrible news. She was very angry and told me, "Call them back and tell them not to do anything until we get there…!" So, I called father back and told him firmly, "Don't you and mother do anything till we get there.!" And I hung up. My father turned to my mother with a smile on his face and said, "Hey, guess what love? The kids are flying over for Christmas and they're paying their own way…!"

Attitude Thought #8

"Staying positive does not mean you are happy all the time
It just means that even on the Hard Days
You know You Always
HAVE A CHOICE"

Chapter Nine

The Healing Power of Gratitude

**"The Healthiest of All Human Emotions
Is Gratitude"**
Zig Ziglar

Wow…! What a powerful quote to start this chapter on Gratitude. I have been so fortunate and grateful for the opportunity to present my "Gratitude With An Attitude" seminar to hundreds of "Treasured Seniors" at numerous Assisted Living and Memory Care Facilities. The love and positive feedback that I get from these presentations is almost overwhelming. They all seem to grasp the intense emotional and healthy benefits that having a Grateful Attitude will create. I hope that I can inspire and motivate everyone reading this chapter to see success of this powerful state of mind.

The simple definition of Gratitude is:

**The Quality of Being Thankful;
The Readiness to Show Appreciation
And
To Return Kindness**

I think everyone loves to get gifts and presents and are so excited to unwrap them. I want you all to look at each day, that we all are so fortunate to receive, as a wonderful gift that we get to rip the wrapping paper off, open it and enjoy. Don't miss the **Gift of Today** with a bitter and sour attitude.

I realize that every day is not always a 'bowl of cherries' and we sometimes get up facing all kinds of unpleasant issues; health, finances, relationships, etc. We can face these challenges with self-pity, bitterness and hate, which will reap some devasting results on our health. OR…! Successfully face them with a clear and winning attitude by being grateful of the things we do have.

"Your Attitude about Your Gratitude Will Determine the Success of Each Day of Your Life"
Fred Kienle

For the last several years I have subsidized my income by presenting seminars and singing engagements to numerous Assisted Living and Memory Care Homes…however, because of this COVID-19 Virus, since March of 2020, these establishments have been in a Lockdown Mode. Well, this cut my finances drastically. I mean you can't get into these homes with a crowbar and I am not sure when I will be able to be able to present my seminars again? I can either sit here and whine, moan, groan, complain and be bitter about the situation – OR – Be Grateful for the things that I DO have and successfully look for other alternatives. I Have A Choice and So Do You…! If I had to, even at 75 years old, I know I can always get a job saying, "Would you like French Fry's with that…?"

Counting your Blessings isn't just a religious statement. It's a statement for everyday life. To many times we fall into the trap of saying that I don't have anything to be grateful or thankful for…Hmmmm…! Really…???

One of my friends was in the dumps and made that same fateful statement to me. I said "Let's make a chart, I'll draw a line down the middle of the paper and put the things that you could be grateful for on the left side of the line, as opposed to the bad things on the right side of the line." He said, "There won't be much on the grateful side." I said, "That's sad." and I added, "I am so sorry to hear that your wife died." He gave me a strange look and said, "Fred, what's wrong with you? My wife is alive and healthy…!" I said, "Oh great…! Let's put that on the Grateful side of the Chart." Then I asked him, "What are you going to do since you lost your job?" "What are you talking about?" He questioned, "I'm still working and have a good job." "Hmmm…" I said, "Has a Good Job. Let's put that on the Grateful side." Then I asked, "Where are you and your family going to live since your house burned down?" "Fred…What is wrong with you?" he asked dumfounded, "My house is standing strong and didn't burn down…!" "Super…!" I exclaimed happily, "Still has a nice home to live in. That should go on the Grateful side.!" I then asked him, "So, are you going to have to take the bus since your car broke down?" He sighed and said, "OKAY…! I see where you are going. You know my car is in good shape and it is something I can be Grateful for." He finally got it and realized that his kids were not on dope and they were healthy. His health was good and so on and so on. If we all took a minute, we can probably fill a few pages with a list of GRATEFUL things we have and have experienced in our life's.

We all face challenges and they can be devasting but if you face them with the attitude of at least being Grateful of the things we do have. The chances of you successfully solving and winning over the issues improve greatly. Your perception of the good and bad things in your life is crucial. Take a minute to digest the following quote by *Amy Weatherly*.

"Some people could be given an entire field of roses and only see the thorns in it. Others could be given a single handful of weeds and see the wildflower in it. Perception is the key component to gratitude. And gratitude a key component to joy."

I read a story about an elderly 90-year-old gentleman named Bill. He was going to move into an assisted living community. Bill was blind and when he arrived at the assisted living home a really nice young lady met him at the door and as she led him down the hall way to his new home she began to tell him all about his room. With great detail she told him about the layout was and how nice the couch was. As she continued to describe the room, Bill interrupted and said in an enthusiastic voice, "It is really Great and I Love It, I really Love It…!" She replied, "Sir, how can you say you Love It when you have not even set foot in it yet…?" Bill smiled and replied, "This is what I have learned through the years. Whether I like my new room or whether I don't like it, does not depend on the layout or how the furniture is arranged. It DOES depend on how my MIND is arranged…!" He continued with a soft voice, "You see young lady, Happiness is something that you decide ahead of time and be Grateful for." Wow…! That says a lot to me. Bill had a choice and he could have been bitter about his new place and find everything about it that he did not like. OR…He could make up his mind to have a Grateful Positive Attitude, finding all the good things about his new dwelling.

When we are handed any situation, how about using that statement;

**"Whether I like my situation or not, the way I will handle it will depend on how
My Mind is Arranged."**

On that list of Positive Affirmations that you are already saying out loud, you can add many of the things you are truly Grateful for. I am not going to bore you with all the names of the notable studies and reports that have proven all the benefits of having a grateful attitude will provide. You can google them on the internet and be overwhelmed with the results. What I want to do is give you an overview of some of these benefits and why it is imperative to do your best, to Have an **"Attitude of Gratitude."**

Grateful people experience fewer aches and pains and report feeling healthier than other people.
Gratitude reduces a multitude of toxic emotions, from envy and resentment to frustration and regret and
effectively increases happiness and reduces depression.
Grateful people, even when given negative feedback, experienced more sensitivity and empathy toward other people and a decreased desire to seek revenge.
Spending a few minutes jotting down a few grateful sentiments before bed can help you sleep better and longer.
Having a Grateful Attitude improves a person's Self Esteem. Which is an essential component to optimal performance.
For years, research has shown gratitude not only reduces stress, but it may also play a major role in overcoming trauma.
Recognizing all that you have to be thankful for —even during the worst times—fosters resilience.

If you don't know who *Nick Vujicic* is, please google him. He was born with NO LEGS and NO ARMS and yet he has become a highly successful Global Motivational Speaker. He is married, has an unbelievable Positive Attitude and is Grateful for everyday he is here on God's Green Earth. If you took some time to read his book *"Life Without Limbs"* it would absolutely STUN you into knowing how Blessed and Grateful you should be. One of his great quotes is:

"I never met a bitter person who was thankful. Or a thankful person who was bitter."
Nick Vujicic

So, don't miss any season in your life being bitter or wishing you had more, complaining about what you don't have. The real joy in life is in the simple things—making memories with your family, riding your bikes together, watching the sunset with your spouse, or staring up at the stars at night. You don't have to have big vacations or lots of money to have fun. Learn to enjoy the simple things in life. Every day is a Gift to unwrap and enjoy.

I love to tell this story I heard about a young boy named Frank. I call it "Zigzagging." He was visiting his uncle at his farm in the country. It was a crisp cool morning and the snow was thick on the ground, Frank and his uncle had been out looking over the property in the woods and his uncle said that it was time to head back to the house. They started trapesing through the snow toward home and Frank went off to the left to look at some ducks swimming in a small pond, then he went over to the right and watched the horses playing and prancing in the cool morning. He then went over to the left again and watched the cows in the pasture and how calm they were. Quickly he again ran to the right over to the big lake and took some time to skip some flat stones over the still water. As he caught up to and joined his uncle at the house, his uncle looked at Frank and said, "Son, I want to teach you a valuable lesson about life." He added, "If you look back over our tracks in the snow you will see the difference in your tracks and mine." The uncle then went on to say, "If you look at your tracks, they zigzag left and right and meander all over the place, while mine are in a straight line heading to the house." "Frank." He explained, "I did not waste time or extra effort and arrived home way before you did." Frank looked back over the tracks and was amazed at the difference and said, "Thanks Uncle, this is the best lesson ever…!" Frank smiled and added, "I still arrived at the same place that you did and look at all the sights and wonderful things I enjoyed along the way."

It's the old cliché that tells us to "Stop and Smell the Roses!" The common sense of this highly used statement should not be overlooked. To many times we get so busy and focused on a goal or destination that we forget to enjoy all the little blessing along our journey. Don't get to busy that you cannot enjoy the taste of the wonderful meal you are eating, the joy of having your pet come up to you wagging their tail wanting you to pet them. How about the beautiful the sound of your kids laughing or playing! Your spouse looking at you with a smile that says I love you. Each day will always be filled to the brim with exciting, wonderful, stimulating things to enjoy…IF…you will just take the time to seek them out.

I like to think of ourselves as being in the manufacturing business. So, if you're going to be in the manufacturing business, your product should be; Laughter, Positive Thoughts, Happy Memories, Pleasant Comments, Positive Affirmations, an Attitude of Gratitude and a Huge Smile on your Face…!

Remember

The Seeds of Discouragement cannot take root in a Grateful Heart.

As you have seen in this chapter having that Attitude of Gratitude is so beneficial to your health, wellbeing and your future. So, Please;

If You Embrace the place where You are, you will be grateful for what You have.

Your happiness is not dependent on your circumstances…it is really dependent on the choices you make. **Abraham Lincoln** said;

"Most people are as happy as they decided to be."

So, I encourage you to:

"Look Back in forgiveness, forward in hope, down in compassion and up in Gratitude."
Zig Ziglar

Time to Laugh

The Barking Dog

Here It was, 2:00 o'clock in the blooming morning. The misses and I had nary a wink of sleep because of the pesky non-stop barking of our neighbors' dog. Finally, I told my wife in despair, "Love, I cannot stand it any longer, this dog has not shut up yet…! It's driving me crazy; I need to go down there and do something!" My wife asked me, "Freddy, what are Ya going ta do?" "I'm not quite sure Love, but I got to do something to shut that yapping dog up." I replied, as I put on my trousers. I headed downstairs as the misses waited anxiously for my return. Well, about 20 minutes later I came back upstairs, took off my trousers and started to get back into the bed. My wife was puzzled and asked me, "What did Ya do Freddy? The stupid dog is still barking his head off." I told her, "I fixed that dog…!" "But Freddy…The crazy dog has not shut up yet, he's still barking as bad as he was before, What Did Ya Do…!" She screamed back at me. I looked her straight in the eye and said, "I went over there, picked that barking dog up, brought him over and put him in OUR Yard." Then, pointing at our neighbor's house, I said, **"Let's See how HE Likes It…???"**

Attitude Thought #9

> "Your Attitude about Your Gratitude
> Will Determine the Success of
> Each Day of Your Life"

Chapter Ten

The Power of Prayer

**"Faith is the Substance of Things Hoped For,
The Evidence of Things Not Seen"**
Hebrew 11:1

The point I want to make so clear in this chapter, is how powerful a person's spirituality can be in their everyday health and in the healing process. Religion and politics are usually subject's that most people will not bring up in a conversation. This chapter is not here to argue theology or different religions. It is here to bring to light how important the role of faith, religion and spirituality can be when it comes to a person's health and wellbeing.

Another point I want to make is, you don't need to be religious to practice the healthful principles laid out by many of the world's religions, because practicing the health tenets espoused by many religions are just good practices and contain good common sense.

So many scientific studies and research have proven the positive value of prayer, fellowshipping and the belief that there is a superior power that we can turn to. They have also proven that so many people who attend religious services live a little longer. Religion has the benefit of empowering an individual through connecting him/her to a community, and to a superior force, which has the ability to give that person some psychological stability. Your spiritual beliefs and principal's will help you stay focused on the good things and give you HOPE. When a person has hope, it lessens depression and when your anxiety level is reduced so is your Blood Pressure. The meditative nature of religious services can lower stress levels by preaching love, forgiveness, hope, and optimism, which foster a positive outlook on life that can translate into good emotional health.

I do understand why doctors and medical professionals always give their patients the "Worst-Case Scenario" concerning their health conditions and the possible outcome. One reason they warn you about the worst-case scenario is so that you will do what you're supposed to do in terms of taking your medication, following their instructions, getting physical therapy or whatever. So many people don't follow the doctor's instructions -- they don't do their physical therapy at home because it hurts, they don't take their meds because they forget, they don't change their diet because they don't want to, they don't exercise because they're lazy, etc. That makes sense and out of a feeling of doom we, as predictable human beings, will be more apt to faithfully adhere to their recommendations. Another reason is to diminish the possibility of these professionals of being sued for not revealing the full possibilities of a person's medical conditions and results of treatments. This is all understandable and all the facts should be made known to all patients. However, I encourage you to never view your health issue or illness as the FINAL outcome or permanent condition, even when the Medical Professionals give you the Worst-Case Scenario. It is up to YOU to take some responsibility in your healing process and actively use your Belief and Faith in God to FIGHT whatever health issues you are facing. I call it:

The God Factor for Your Health

In earlier chapters I have talked about focusing on your health issues by saying positive affirmations. I am a Christian by faith and believe in Jesus Christ. I use many Biblical verses and principals when I am addressing any of my health issues. You should use whatever your belief system has in the area of healing and health. Since I do not know what sayings and prayers other religions have so, I will use, as examples, the verses from the King James Version of the Bible that I have successfully used in helping me get through health issues that I have faced.

When I was diagnosed with Debilitating Rheumatoid Arthritis and they gave me all the gruesome probable outcome of deformed joints and the pain I would incur, it really scared me. I had to stop and dig deep into my soul to remind myself that there are alternative prescriptions that too many medical professionals leave out of your healing possibilities. They are:

PRAYER, BELIEF and FAITH IN GOD

It was good to know all the possible negatives that I could face, because along with following the doctor's advice, taking the medication as prescribed, it also gave me actual targets to focus on with prayer and positive defensive affirmations!

I would say out loud, several times a day "In the Name of Jesus Christ"
1. I cast out this infirmity of Arthritis from My body.
2. I will fight off this Arthritis and My bones will not be deformed.
3. I rebuke this pain and swelling in My Joints.
4. My body will respond favorably to all the recommendations from my doctors.

I would repeat the Bible Verse *Mark 11:23-25* over and over:

²³ For verily I say unto you, That whosoever shall say unto this mountain, Be thou removed, and be thou cast into the sea; and shall not doubt in his heart, but shall believe that those things which he saith shall come to pass; he shall have whatsoever he saith.
²⁴ Therefore I say unto you, What things soever ye desire, when ye pray, believe that ye receive them, and ye shall have them.
²⁵ And when ye stand praying, **FORGIVE,** *if ye have ought against any: that your Father also which is in heaven may forgive you your trespasses.*

If you noticed I put the word Forgive in Bold letters and underlined it. The reason is that when you harbor unforgiveness toward anything or anybody, it is like taking a dose of poison on a regular basis. Unforgiveness, in 99.999999999% of the time only effects the person that harbors it. Most of the time the person the hate and unforgiveness it is directed toward, doesn't even know it or feel it. So, why waste your energy, emotion and feelings toward something that will drastically and negatively affect your Health. When you are in a forgiving mode your body will function more effectively; less stress, lower blood pressure, better heart rate, boosted immune factor…and so on and so forth. I think you get the full picture.

Forgiveness is one of the best Prescriptions
For Healing so many Issues
Including our Health

One of my favorite Bible Verses about healing is captured in *1 Peter 2:24*

²⁴ Who his own self bare our sins in his own body on the tree, that we, being dead to sins, should live unto righteousness: **_by whose stripes ye were healed._**

This wonderful verse tells me that because of Gods Mercy and Grace with the fact that Jesus Christ was Crucified, Buried and then rose again in Resurrection Power. I (We) was/were ALREADY Healed 2000 Years ago. WOW…! This gives everything in my spiritual and physical body such a Boost for My HOPE & FAITH that there is a Superior Source that I can rely on which will overcome Satan and the Evil of this world and support a Positive Outcome.

Throughout my life, just by saying and repeating these verses and positive affirmations out loud when health issues have attacked me, I know for a fact that I have always healed faster, quicker and more completely than I would have without them. You have to actively and consciously say and do these things. I like to reference the 23rd Psalms verse 4:

⁴ Yea, though I walk **_through_** *the valley of the shadow of death, I will fear no evil: for thou art with me; thy rod and thy staff they comfort me.*

The key word in this verse is "THROUGH." Too many times when an illness or issue rears its ugly head, we kinda pitch a tent, set up camp and just worry, fret and wring our hands about it. This verse tells us to walk THROUGH it and HE will help us. So, get up off your duff and fight the illness with everything you have.,

I could fill several pages with scriptural verses that I use but I recommend that YOU find the verses and religious saying that will fit your unique health situations. Remember you don't need to be religious to practice the healthful principles laid out by many of the world's religions.

I will close this chapter with how I began it by reminding you how powerful a person's spirituality can be in their everyday health and in the healing process.

Time to Laugh

Spell a Word

One day a lady went to Heaven and walked up to the Pearly Gates, where Saint Peter was standing and she said, "Hello, I'd like to get into Heaven, what do I need to do?" Saint Peter answered, "You just need to spell a word." "What word would that be?" she asked? "Any word you would like." He replied. "Really, Any word?" She remarked. "Yep, any word you want." She said "How about LOVE?" and she spelled out "LOVE" ... Saint Peter said, "Great, you can go on into Heaven!" then he quickly asked, "Could you do a favor for me and watch the Pearly Gate while I take a short break?" She said, "Sure, what do I need to do?" Saint Peter said, "You just need to ask the people like I asked you, to spell a word, any word they would like, and that would allow them to get into Heaven." She said "OKAY." And he went off on his break.

Not long after he left a new lady came up to the gate and asked what she need to do to get into Heaven? The lady watching the gate told her, all she had to do was spell a word, any word she wanted. "Wow" the new lady responded and chose to spell FAITH. She spelled it and went on into Heaven. It was not long before a new person came up to the gate. The lady was appalled that it was her divorced husband. She exclaimed, "What are you doing here?" He remarked sarcastically, "I am here to get into Heaven, what do I need to do?" She looked at him with a frown and said, "You need to spell a word." He then asked, "What word would that be?" And with a Huge Grin on her face, she replied, **"CZECHOSLOVAKIA….!!!"**

Attitude Thought #10

> **"Faith is the Substance of Things Hoped For,
> The Evidence of Things Not Seen"**
> *Hebrew 11:1*

Chapter Eleven

Closing Summary

"If You Have Your Health – You Have Everything…!"

I opened this book with that statement from my grandmother and I believe it is fitting that I close with the same statement. When you are healthy "The World is Your Oyster" and when your health is in poor condition, the world can be depressing, sad and scary. I hope this book has opened up some new avenues of options, principals and opportunities to help you live a Longer, Happier and Healthier Life. The choice is yours and yours alone to follow the advice laid down on these pages. I believe that a person's ATTITIDE plays such an important part in EVERY THING we do. Especially when it comes to our HEALTH. Let me finish with the following combined quotes and statements:

**If you Change Your Attitude, you can Change Your Health
Because
The Attitude and State of Mind that You use to confront any of the
Treatments, Surgeries, Therapy and Recommendations
Your physician prescribes for You,
WILL
Have a dramatic effect on the Outcome and Success of Your Recovery
So,
If You work in conjunction with Your mind and body,
by having a Better Attitude,
You will help Amplify the Natural Healing process
Already inherent within Your own body
So,
I am convinced that
Life is 10% of what happens to You
And
90% of how You React to It.
So, Let's**

Bring Our Self into the Healing Process
By Staying Positive.
However,
Staying positive does not mean you are happy all the time
It just means that even on the Hard Days
You know You Always
HAVE A CHOICE
To
Change Your Got To's into Your Get To's
By
Speaking Out Loud, Positive Affirmations that will Enhance your Health
Because
Self-Talk is One of the most powerful means of Communication
And it can either
Empower You or Defeat You
So Be
Grateful that You have a Choice.
Zig Ziglar said
"The Healthiest of All Human Emotions Is Gratitude"
And
The Seeds of Discouragement cannot take root in a Grateful Heart.
Remember
The GOOD thing about this is ---
It's totally up to you...!
And
The BAD thing about this is ---
It's Totally up to YOU...!
All of this should really tell You that
YOU ARE IN CHARGE OF THE CHOICES YOU MAKE
It's Not a Roll of the Dice, it is a Conscious Effort
To
Change Your Attitude
And
Change Your Health
Because
"If You Have Your Health – You Have Everything…!"

God Bless and Thank You,
Fred Kienle

About the Author

Fred Kienle has come up through the ranks learning how to understand and deal with people and personalities through trial and error...! He attended Texas Western College (UTEP) in El Paso, Texas. He was a musician/recording artist for 25 years playing in a myriad of diverse clubs and concerts. He was a licensed electrician and has owned several small businesses. For over 22 years, he worked for a major corporation in Dallas, Texas. He taught and trained hundreds of employees in Six Sigma, Ethics and Safety. He has been certified as a Six Sigma Expert and specializes in Team Building and Team Facilitation. Fred has been self-employed since 2006 as a Published Author, Speaker, Consultant and Singer/Entertainer. He conducts a series of "Attitude Seminars" for Corporations, Businesses, Schools, Churches, Cities and hundreds of

Assisted Living/Memory Care establishments in the Dallas / Fort Worth Metroplex. He is also a Licensed Health Insurance Agent specializing in Medicare Solutions. He resides in Texas with his Wife of 50 Years and their two Dogs.

HEALTH WITH AN ATTITUDE

HWAA
Fred D. Kienle © 2021

Made in the USA
Coppell, TX
05 June 2022